The Gap

FOUR QUESTIONS BETWEEN A GUESS AND A FORTUNE

SRIRAM SARAVANAN

Author of
THE GAME OF PERCENTAGE and THE EFFORTLESS INVESTOR

ISBN: 9798191822204

Important Notice

This book is for educational and informational purposes only. It is not financial advice.

The author is not a registered financial advisor, portfolio manager, dealer, or investment professional in any jurisdiction, and nothing in this book should be treated as a personal recommendation to buy, sell, or hold any security. Investing carries risk, including the risk of losing money. Past performance does not predict future results.

Before acting on anything you read here, consult a qualified professional who knows your individual financial situation.

A full disclaimer appears at the back of this book.

By reading further,
you confirm that you have read and accepted it.

Dedication

To my parents,
who spent what they did not have so that I would never have to count the way they counted.

And to my wife,
who has never once asked me to be anything other than the man I was still becoming.

I have written three books about building a fortune.

You are the three I never had to build.

THE GAP

CONTENTS

Foreword

There are only four questions in the stock market.

Not forty. Not four hundred. Four.

- **WHAT TO BUY?**
- **WHEN TO BUY?**
- **HOW MUCH TO BUY?**
- **WHEN TO SELL?**

Everything else is one of those four questions wearing a costume. Every headline. Every podcast. Every confident voice on your screen pointing at a green arrow. The costume changes daily. The questions never change at all.

Most people who lose money in the market do not lose it because they picked the wrong company. They lose it because they never answered these four questions on purpose. So they answer them by accident instead, at eleven at night, on a phone, on the strength of something a stranger said with great confidence.

I know this, because that was me.

THE DELUSION OF WINNING

I started investing in 2019, and I started the way almost everyone starts. I bought what I could see.

There was a logic to it, and I want to be fair to my younger self here, because he was trying. I bought the companies whose products were already in my life. The milk in my fridge. The steel going into the building at the end of my street. The cars sitting in traffic in front of me every morning. If a business was woven into ordinary life, I reasoned, the business must be sound.

That is not the worst instinct a beginner can have. It is simply not a strategy. It is pattern recognition wearing a lab coat.

Then I did something worse. I started trading.

For a while I paid a man to send me tips. He would message in the morning. Buy this at the open, sell it before the close, and there was always a reason, and the reason was always excellent. I spent my working hours with a chart open in another window, feeling the specific nausea of a person whose money is moving without asking him first.

Some days I made money. Some days I gave it back. On the good days I felt clever and on the bad days I felt unlucky, and it did not occur to me for a long time that this was suspicious. Clever and unlucky are not opposites. They are the same feeling wearing different weather.

Eventually I stopped, and I stopped for the right reason. Trading was not investing. Trading was a slot machine with a research report stapled to the front of it, and I had been feeding it with a straight face.

So I got serious. I read. I learned what a balance sheet was actually telling me. I bought companies I could defend in an argument, real businesses with real earnings and long histories, the sort of names that make people nod when you say them at dinner. By any reasonable measure, this was an upgrade.

And I still got it wrong, because having bought good companies, I could not leave them alone.

I switched. Something would run and I would take the profit. Something else would start to look better and the money would follow it there. I was managing a portfolio the way an anxious cook manages a pot, lifting the lid every few minutes to check on it, letting the heat out every single time, and then wondering why dinner was late.

By the end of it, I had made money. Real money.

I remember the number and I remember exactly how it felt to look at it.

It felt like winning.

THE AFTERNOON THE NUMBER CHANGED

Then one day, I sat down and did something I had never bothered to do properly.

I turned my winnings into a percentage.

Not the profit. The rate. I took what I had earned, subtracted the trading fees, subtracted the taxes, divided what was left by the money I had put in, and looked at what came back.

Seven percent. In a good year, maybe ten.

The number did not hurt immediately. I want to be honest about that. For a few seconds it was just a number, sitting there, being reasonable. Seven percent is not a shameful figure. Seven percent is fine.

Then it arrived.

I was living in India then, where interest rates run far above anything you will see in North America. A fixed deposit at an ordinary bank, the local cousin of a GIC in

Canada or a CD in the United States, was paying about seven percent that year. Guaranteed. No research. No screens. No opinions required. You sign a form at a counter and then you go and live your life.

Three years. Annual reports I had read at midnight. Earnings calls. Charts. The rumours and the reversals and the small daily weather of the market, all of it absorbed, all of it carried.

And all I had managed to achieve was a tie with a piece of paper you sign at a bank

I sat with that for a long time. It was not the loss that got me, because there was no loss. That was exactly the problem. I had won, technically, measurably, in every way I had been counting. The money was there. I could point at it.

The money had told me I was winning. The percentage told me what I had actually done with three years of my life.

That afternoon is the reason I have written three books instead of none, because I finally understood that my mistake was not a stock-picking mistake at all. It was a measurement mistake. I had been reading my own results in the wrong unit, and a wrong unit will let you celebrate anything.

Here is the lesson in its smallest form, and I would ask you to carry it with you through the rest of this book.

A profit of a thousand dollars means nothing by itself. On five thousand invested, it is twenty percent (*superb*). On a hundred thousand invested, it is one percent (quite a disaster).

Same number. Same smile on your face. Opposite lives.

Dollars flatter. *Percentages do not.*

I wrote my first book, *The Game of Percentage*, about exactly that, because once you start reading the world in percentages you cannot stop, and you begin to see how much of personal finance is built on people not doing it. Inflation stops being a news item and becomes a hurdle you must clear before you have earned a single thing. A management fee stops being a service charge and becomes a permanent subtraction from your compounding, taken first, every year, forever. Positive returns and making money stop being the same sentence.

Then I moved to *Canada* in 2022, and I learned that the country changes and the mistake does not.

THE WOMAN IN THE GYM

The gym in my condo building used to be small. Two treadmills, one bike, a rack of weights, and a window that looked out at the gazebo.

I go at the same time every afternoon, and so did she. Sixties. Warm, quick, the kind of person who learns your name in the first week and asks after your mother for the next three years. She took the bike. I took the treadmill. We built the particular friendship you build with someone you see every single day and know almost nothing about.

Eventually she found out what I wrote about. And after that, the conversation turned to money.

She told me her portfolio was returning five and a half percent a year. She said it the way you announce a grandchild's grades, still pedalling, pleased with herself. Then she told me what she paid the people who managed it, and that part she said more quietly, without slowing down, the way people mention a cost they have already decided not to think about.

I asked her what inflation was running at that year.

She smiled and said she didn't know. She said it lightly. It was closer to seven.

I did the arithmetic on the treadmill while she talked about her daughter. Five and a half, less the fee, call it four. Against seven. Every year. And the arrangement, she had mentioned once, cheerfully, had been running for eleven years.

Here is the thing about losing money this way.

There is no crash. Nothing appears on the news. Nobody calls you. Your statement arrives, and the number at the bottom is larger than it was last quarter, and you feel the small warm satisfaction of a person whose plan is working. Nothing screams. Nothing breaks. The number climbs, and the money buys less, and the two facts sit side by side on the same page, politely, for eleven years, and never once introduce themselves.

She had been quietly emptied by a process that sends a friendly letter every three months.

And she was happy about it. That is the part I have never been able to put down.

She was happy, she was proud of it, she had brought it up herself, and I was the only person in that room who knew, and I had the length of a treadmill program to decide whether to say so.

I thought about my seven percent. I thought about three years spent earning what a form at a bank counter would have handed me for nothing.

I recognised her. That is the worst of it.

Different country, different product, different decade, same person, and nobody had told either of us.

The next afternoon, she was on the bike at the usual time, and so was I.

Which Brings Us Here

That conversation became my second book, *The Effortless Investor*, about an industry that has made the market look complicated because your feeling unqualified is the product. Two books in, I thought I was done. I had written about how to measure. I had written about what the industry does not volunteer.

But the conversations kept coming. Friends. Strangers. Men at parties who found out what I did and immediately wanted to tell me about the one stock they had bought and how it was doing.

And after enough of them, I noticed something.
Every one of those conversations was one of four questions. Not most. Every one.

Should I buy this one? That is *what to buy.*

Is now a good time, or should I wait for a dip? That is *when to buy.*

How much should I put in? That is *how much to buy.*

It's up thirty percent, should I take the profit? That is *when to sell.*

That is the whole universe of investing anxiety.

It has four rooms in it and no more, and everyone I spoke to was wandering between them in the dark, at speed, in a panic, without ever noticing there were only four.

Nobody had laid them out plainly, in order, and shown these people what a good answer looks like. So they improvised all four at once, under pressure, using information supplied by people who profit from their confusion.

That is *the Gap*.

It is not a gap in intelligence. The people in those conversations were engineers and nurses and business owners, entirely competent everywhere else in their lives. It is a gap in sequence.

They answer the first question with reasoning that belongs to the third. They answer the fourth with pure feeling. Then they look at results that seem random and conclude the market is random.

Results that feel random usually are.

WHAT THIS BOOK WILL DO

Four chapters. One question each. In this order, for a reason, because each answer narrows the next the way a good decision should.

I am not going to give you a stock tip. I am not going to tell you about a company that is about to explode. If that is what you came for, put this down now and keep your money, and I mean that without any hostility at all.

And I am not much interested in you memorising my answers either. Borrowed answers do not survive contact with a falling market. What I want is for you to finish this book unable to buy anything, ever again, without hearing four questions in your head first, in order, in your own voice.

What I am going to do is give you four answers you can hold for the next forty years without revisiting them, and explain them well enough that you understand why they work. A rule you do not understand is a rule you will abandon the first time the market frightens you.

And it will frighten you. That is not a risk. That is a schedule.

One more thing before we start.

By the time you reach the end of this book, you will be down to three questions.

One of these four is going to leave. It will not be answered. It will dissolve, quietly, once you understand what the others are really doing, and I suspect you will be surprised by which one goes.

I am not going to tell you. That would spoil it.

Let's begin.

THE GAP

QUESTION NUMBER 1

–

WHAT TO BUY?

THE GAP

"GIVE ME SIX HOURS TO CHOP DOWN A TREE AND I WILL SPEND THE FIRST FOUR SHARPENING THE AXE."

ABRAHAM LINCOLN

Except he didn't say it.

Lincoln died in 1865. The earliest version of that line anyone has been able to find in print appeared in 1956, in a book about agricultural education, where it was credited to an unnamed woodsman. Somewhere in the following decades it acquired a top hat and a beard, and now it lives on coffee mugs.

I am opening a chapter about how to choose an investment with a quotation that millions of intelligent people have repeated, published, and built presentations around without once asking where it came from. I can think of no better way to begin.

Because that is the whole problem in miniature. The line sounds right. It is attributed to someone credible. Everyone around you is repeating it. And nobody checks, because checking feels unnecessary when a claim is already this popular.

Now replace the quotation with a stock.

The advice is worth keeping, incidentally. Somebody did write something very close to it, and we know exactly who. In 1901, Josiah Strong published a book called The Times and Young Men, and in it he wrote: time spent in sharpening the axe may well be spared from swinging it. Less quotable. Considerably more verifiable.

So let us sharpen the axe.

THE QUESTION UNDERNEATH THE QUESTION

When somebody asks me what they should buy, they almost never mean what they are asking.

What they mean is: tell me something that will go up. They have already decided that the goal is to go up, and they are treating "up" as a single, undifferentiated direction. Up is good. More up is better. Find me the most up.

But up is not a direction. Up is a rate. And a rate is only meaningful against something.

I laboured this point for an entire book, so I will not relitigate it here beyond what this chapter needs.

THE GAP

My first book, *The Game of Percentage*, exists because I spent three years feeling successful and was wrong about it, and the only thing standing between me and the truth was a division sign. If you have not read it, the argument compresses to this: a return means nothing until you know what it beat.

Which means before you can answer what to buy, you have to answer a question that comes before it. Not what should I buy, but:

WHAT DOES MY MONEY HAVE TO BEAT BEFORE I HAVE EARNED ANYTHING AT ALL?

That number exists. It is knowable. It is specific to the country you live in and the year you are reading this. And almost nobody calculates it, which is why almost everybody is satisfied with results that should horrify them.

Let me show you how to build it.

THE FLOOR

There are three floors, stacked. You have to clear all three, in order, before the word "returns" means anything.

FLOOR ONE: WHAT YOUR MONEY EARNS FOR DOING NOTHING.

Not investing. Sitting. In a savings account, at the bank you already use, requiring no decision and no courage.

In Canada, at the time I am writing this, the average ongoing rate across dozens of savings accounts is under one percent, and at the largest banks the standard savings rate can be as low as a fifth of one percent. Some online banks, covered by the identical government deposit insurance, pay several times that. Same protection. Same access. Multiples of the return.

I want you to sit with that for a second, because it tells you something about this entire industry that no chart will. Two products, identical in risk, identical in insurance, differing by a factor of ten in what they pay you. The only variable is whether you ever looked.

FLOOR TWO: WHAT YOUR MONEY EARNS FOR TAKING NO RISK AT ALL.

In Canada this is a Guaranteed Investment Certificate. In the United States it is a certificate of deposit.

You hand over the money, you agree not to touch it for a fixed term, and the return is contractually guaranteed.

As I write, the best one-year GIC in Canada pays about 3.6 percent. The best five-year is a little over four. These are not investments in any meaningful sense. They are the price of parking.

But they matter enormously, because they are your true zero. Any strategy that requires research, attention, courage, and risk, and delivers less than this, is not merely disappointing. It is irrational. You have accepted risk and received nothing for it.

This is the floor I failed to clear for three years without noticing.

FLOOR THREE: WHAT YOUR MONEY MUST EARN TO STAY THE SAME SIZE.

Inflation.

Whatever the official figure is in your country on the day you read this, go and look it up. I am deliberately not printing a number here, because a number would date this book and because I want you in the habit. It takes ninety seconds. Your central bank or national statistics office publishes it.

Then understand what it means. If inflation runs at three percent and your money earns three percent, you have earned nothing. You have stood still while walking. Your account balance grew and your life did not improve by a single dollar.

And here is the part that made a woman on an exercise bike smile at me and say she didn't know: inflation is not subtracted from your returns on any statement you will ever receive. There is no line item. Nobody sends a letter. Your balance goes up and your purchasing power goes down, and both facts are true at once, and only one of them is printed anywhere.

NOW STACK THEM

So here is your actual question, the one hiding under what should I buy:

I live in this country. Doing nothing pays me roughly this. Taking zero risk pays me roughly this. Standing still costs me roughly this. Therefore, before I accept a single unit of risk, my target is a number meaningfully above all three.

Write it down. Actually write it. Not because the number is magic, but because a written number is a thing you can be wrong about, and a vague ambition is not.

Once you have it, something clarifying happens. Most of what you were considering disqualifies itself immediately, and you have not had to develop an opinion about a single company.

That is the axe, sharpened. Now we can swing it.

The Answer:

YOU SHOULD BUY THE WHOLE MARKET, THROUGH A BROAD, LOW-COST, INDEX-TRACKING FUND, AND YOU SHOULD KEEP BUYING IT.

That is the answer. That is the entire answer to the first question, and if you closed the book here you would already be ahead of most of the people you know.

I am aware of how that lands. You came here for a chapter about how to choose, and I have told you not to choose. Some part of you is already assembling the objection, and it probably sounds like: but surely I can do better than average.

The rest of this chapter is about why that sentence is the most expensive sentence in personal finance, and why "average" is one of the great mislabellings of our time.

WHY NOT A COMPANY

Let us take your instinct seriously, because it deserves better than mockery.

You want to own a business. Not a basket, a business. Something you understand, whose products you can hold, whose CEO you have opinions about. This is not a stupid desire. It is the oldest form of ownership there is, and it built most of the fortunes in history.

The problem is not that picking companies is hard. The problem is what the distribution of outcomes actually looks like, and almost nobody has been shown it.

In 2018, a finance professor named Hendrik Bessembinder published a paper in the Journal of Financial Economics with a title that reads like a trick question: Do Stocks Outperform Treasury Bills? He took every common stock that had appeared in the main US database since 1926, tens of thousands of them, and calculated what each one actually returned over its entire listed life.

Here is what he found.

Four out of every seven of those stocks returned less over their lifetimes than one-month Treasury bills. Less than the most boring instrument in existence. Not less than the market. Less than cash.

The median stock lost money.

And then the finding that should reorganise how you think about this permanently: the best-performing four percent of listed companies account for the entire net gain of the US stock market since 1926. The other ninety-six percent, collectively, matched Treasury bills. Narrow it further and it gets stranger. Around ninety companies, roughly one third of one percent of everything that ever listed, produced more than half of all the wealth the market ever created. Five firms alone account for a tenth of it.

Bessembinder later extended the work through 2022. Of the twenty-eight thousand US stocks that ever listed, more than fifty-eight percent destroyed shareholder wealth rather than creating it. Seventy-two companies, about a quarter of one percent, explain half of everything.

Now think about what that means for you, standing in front of a screen, choosing one.

The market's famous long-run return is real. But it is not distributed the way you imagine. It is not that most stocks do fine and a few do badly. It is that almost all stocks do badly or indifferently, and a vanishingly small number do so spectacularly well that they carry the entire index on their backs.

The index return is an average in the same way that a room containing you and a billionaire has an average net worth of half a billion dollars. Technically true. Descriptively useless. Everything depends on which body you are.

Bessembinder ran the simulation that makes this concrete. If you had picked a single stock at random and held it for the full ninety years, you would have underperformed the market in ninety-six cases out of a hundred. You would have underperformed a Treasury bill in seventy-three.

This is the number I wish somebody had put in front of me in 2019.

Because notice what it does to the phrase I can do better than average. When the average is produced by a handful of extreme winners hidden inside a crowd of losers, beating the average does not require being slightly above the crowd. It requires holding the extremes.

And the extremes are, by construction, almost impossible to identify in advance, because if they were identifiable in advance they would not be cheap enough to become extremes.

You are not competing to be better than average. You are competing to find the four percent, while ninety-six percent of the field looks, from the outside, extremely similar.

And here is the thing about buying the whole market: it means you own the four percent. Automatically. Without knowing which ones they are. You will also own the ninety-six percent, and they will drag, and it will feel inefficient, and it is exactly this inefficiency that guarantees you never miss the companies that matter.
You are not settling for the average. You are buying the winners at the price of also buying the losers, which is the only reliable way anyone has ever found to own them.

WHY NOT A MANAGER

The obvious reply is that you should not pick stocks yourself, but you should hire somebody whose job it is.

I wrote a whole book about why this fails, so I will be brief here and point you to The Effortless Investor if you want the full autopsy. But the headline deserves repeating, because it is the single most ignored body of evidence in retail finance.

Since 2002, S&P Dow Jones Indices has published a scorecard called SPIVA, which does something the fund industry would never do voluntarily. It compares active fund managers against the index they claim to beat, adjusts for the funds that quietly died along the way, and publishes the result every year, in every major market.

The results are not close, and they have not been close for twenty-five years.

In 2025, seventy-nine percent of active large-cap US equity funds underperformed the S&P 500. That was the fourth-worst year for active management in the entire history of the scorecard, but a bad year for them is not the point. The point is what happens when you extend the horizon. Over fifteen years, roughly ninety percent of large-cap funds underperformed. Over twenty, about ninety-two percent. And across every equity and bond category they measure, the underperformance rate rises as the time period lengthens.

At fifteen years, there was not a single category in which most active managers beat their benchmark.

Now hold that next to your own situation, because you are not investing for one year. You are investing for thirty. You are shopping in exactly the aisle where the failure rate is highest.

The predictable objection is that you will simply choose a good manager. So S&P publishes a second scorecard for that, tracking whether managers who did well keep doing well. They took the funds that finished in the top half in 2021 and followed them. Over the next four years, only a handful stayed in the top half. For large-cap funds specifically, the persistence was worse than random chance would predict, which is a polite way of saying that past performance in this industry is not merely an unreliable signal, it may be a slightly misleading one.

That is the finding that ends the argument for me. It means the good years were mostly luck, and luck does not renew.

In fairness, and because I would rather you trusted this book than agreed with it, the active management industry disputes SPIVA's methodology. A study sponsored by the Investment Adviser Association argued in 2026 that the scorecard understates how active funds perform.

You should know that objection exists. You should also notice that no version of the counter-argument produces a world in which most managers beat the index over fifteen years, and that the objection is funded by the people being measured.

And underneath all of it sits the fee. In Canada, the asset-weighted average expense ratio across all mutual fund series is close to one and a half percent a year. Broad index funds are available for a fraction of that, in some cases under a fifth of one percent. That difference is not a rounding error, it is the whole game, and it is deducted automatically, first, in good years and bad, and never appears as a line on your statement.

Go back to the floors we built. A manager charging one and a half percent has to beat the index by one and a half percent, every single year, just to draw level with the thing you could have bought yourself for almost nothing.

Ninety percent of them do not manage it over fifteen years. And you have to pick which ten percent will, in advance, using a signal that S&P has demonstrated does not persist.

What "Broad" Actually Means

So: an index fund. Which one?

Here the honest answer has a range in it, and I would rather give you the range than a false precision.

There are two defensible positions, and they disagree with each other in an interesting way.

The first is to own one country's largest companies, most commonly the five hundred largest in the United States. This has been, for a century, an extraordinary bet. The long-run record is roughly ten percent a year before inflation. The companies inside it earn revenue globally, so you are less concentrated than the label suggests. And it is the single most liquid, most competitive, most heavily analysed pool of businesses in human history.

The second is to own the entire world. Every developed market, every emerging one, thousands of companies across dozens of countries, weighted by size, rebalancing itself as the world changes without you doing anything.

The argument for the first is performance. The argument for the second is humility.

I hold the second view, and I want to be honest that it costs me something. Over the last fifteen years the American market has beaten the world, and a globally diversified investor has watched a US-only investor do better, repeatedly, and has had to sit still through it.

Here is why I sit still anyway.

Every single person who ever lost a fortune by concentrating did so in a market that had recently been winning. That is not a coincidence, it is the mechanism. Concentration only ever looks wise in hindsight and only ever looks foolish in advance, and the sequence in which those two feelings arrive is the entire risk.

Japan is the case nobody in North America talks about. In 1989 the Japanese stock market was the largest in the world by capitalisation, its companies were studied in every business school, and its dominance was treated as a structural fact rather than a phase. An investor who concentrated there, entirely reasonably, waited more than thirty years to get back to even.

Nothing in the data tells me the United States is Japan. Everything in the data tells me that being certain about which country wins the next forty years is a claim nobody has ever been in a position to make.

So, the practical version is this. If you buy a single broad global equity fund, you have answered the question completely and permanently. One product. Every market. Automatically rebalanced. Nothing to maintain.

If you prefer the American market, buy that instead, and understand exactly what you have chosen: a bet with a magnificent record and a geography attached.

What I would ask you not to do is buy several funds without checking what is inside them. This is the most common self-inflicted wound among people who have just discovered index investing. They buy a global fund, then a US fund because the US has done well, then a technology fund because technology has done well, and they believe they have built diversification. They have not. They have bought the same forty companies three times at three different weights, paid three sets of fees for the privilege, and constructed something they cannot describe in a sentence.

Every fund publishes its holdings. If you cannot say in one plain sentence what you own and why the second fund is there, you own one fund too many.

What You Should Actually Expect

Now the part most books skip, and the part I consider the most important in this chapter, because everything in the last chapter of this book depends on it.

What number should you expect?

You are going to see extraordinary figures quoted. Broad funds launched in the last decade will show returns of fifteen percent a year or more since inception, and those figures are accurate. They are also measurements of one of the strongest stretches in market history, taken over a window shorter than a mortgage.

The long record says something calmer. Over roughly a century, the American market has returned about ten percent a year with dividends reinvested, and closer to seven after inflation.

Ten. Not fifteen.

Now look at how that ten arrived, because the arithmetic mean hides the experience entirely.

The 1950s returned nineteen and a half percent a year.

The 2000s lost money, minus zero point nine percent annually across the entire decade, which after inflation was minus three point four.

The 1970s returned a nominal six percent and lost purchasing power the whole time. Inside those decades sit years like 1931, down forty-seven percent. 2008, down thirty-eight. 2022, down nineteen.

The ten percent is real. It is also an average of experiences that ranged from euphoric to unbearable, and you do not get to choose which decade you are assigned.

So here is my promise to you, and I have thought carefully about how to word it, because a promise made wrongly at the start of a book is what makes people give up in the middle of one.

If you buy the whole market, at low cost, and keep buying it for decades, you should expect something in the region of ten percent a year before inflation, arriving in the most uneven and psychologically punishing sequence you can imagine. You should expect at least one decade that feels like a failure. You should expect years that erase a third of everything you have.

That is not a warning attached to the plan. That is the plan.

I am telling you this now, in the first chapter, deliberately. Because in a few years the market might fall hard, and on that morning the only thing standing between you and a catastrophic decision will be whether you were told the truth at the start. If somebody promised you fifteen percent a year, a bad decade feels like betrayal, and betrayal justifies quitting. If you were told to expect exactly this, it feels like the schedule.

Now put ten percent, arriving unevenly, next to the floors we built at the start of this chapter. Against a guaranteed 3.6, against inflation, against a savings account paying a fifth of one percent. Over thirty years, that gap is not a difference in outcome. It is a difference in what kind of life is available to you at the end.

You do not need fifteen. You never needed fifteen. Fifteen is the number that makes people gamble, and gambling is what put them here.

Sharpening Your Own Axe

I have given you the answer to the first question, and I've

given you the evidence. There is one thing left, and it is the part that cannot be outsourced to a study.

The axe is not the fund. The axe is you.

Everything in this chapter assumed something I have not yet asked you to verify, which is that the money you are about to invest is money you can genuinely leave alone through a decade like the 2000s.

Because the strategy in this chapter has never failed over a long enough horizon. But it fails constantly over short ones, and the reason it fails is never the fund. It is that the money was needed, or the fear was larger than expected, or the plan was made by a version of the person who had not yet watched a third of it disappear.

So before you buy anything, three honest questions.

When do you need this money? Not when would you like it. When do you need it. If the honest answer is under five years, nothing in this chapter applies to that money and you should be looking at the second floor we built, the guaranteed one. Equities are not for a horizon you can see the end of.

What does a forty percent fall feel like to you? Not in theory. Take whatever you are planning to invest, multiply it by point six, and look at the number. That is a real morning that will really happen. If that number makes you feel ill, you are not choosing the wrong fund, you are choosing the wrong amount, and that is the third question in this book, which we will come to.

What do you actually know about yourself? I knew, in 2019, that I could not leave a position alone. I had evidence. I did it repeatedly. I nevertheless built a strategy that required me to leave positions alone, because I was designing for the person I wished I were.

The reason the whole-market answer works is not that it is clever. It is that it is the only answer that survives contact with an ordinary person having an ordinary bad year.

Sharpen the axe. Find out what you can carry. Then buy the boring thing, and buy it for the rest of your life.

Which brings us to the question everyone asks next, and asks with a particular note of anxiety in their voice, because they have been told that this one is where the real skill lies.

THE GAP

QUESTION NUMBER 2

–

WHEN TO BUY?

"TIME IN THE MARKET BEATS TIMING THE MARKET."

AN INVESTING PROVERB

Nobody knows who said that one either. It has been credited to at least four different famous investors, none of whom appear to have said it, which by now you will recognise as the standard condition of investment wisdom. The line survives on merit rather than parentage.

And it happens to be true, which puts it slightly ahead of most things said about the stock market.

THE QUESTION WITH THE ANXIOUS VOICE

Of the four questions in this book, this is the one people ask with a particular tightness in their voice.

Should I wait for a dip?

Is this a good entry point?

The market's at an all-time high, should I hold off?

I have had this conversation perhaps two hundred times. It is always the same conversation, and the person asking it always believes they are asking about the market. They are not. They are asking for permission to postpone a decision that frightens them, and they would like the permission to arrive dressed as strategy.

I say this with sympathy, because I did it for years. Waiting feels like doing something. It feels prudent, even sophisticated. You are not being passive, you are being patient. You are watching. You are waiting for your moment.

The trouble is that waiting is not a neutral act. It is a position. When you sit in cash waiting for a better price, you have made a specific prediction about the near future, and you are being paid a savings account rate to be right about it.

So let me give you the answer immediately, because this chapter is going to be shorter on suspense than the last one.

The Answer:

NOW.

And then again on your next payday.

And the one after that. For the next several years, without ever again asking whether it is a good time.

That is the whole answer. The correct entry point is the moment you have money you will not need for a long time, and the correct frequency is every time that happens, permanently, on a schedule you set once and then stop revisiting.

You may notice this is not a strategy so much as the abolition of a strategy. That is deliberate. The rest of this chapter is about why the alternative, the one where you use judgement, is not the sophisticated option. It is the expensive one.

Why Waiting Requires Two Miracles

Here is the part almost nobody works out, and it is pure arithmetic rather than opinion.

When you decide to wait for a dip, you have not made one prediction. You have made two, and they are independent, and you need both of them to be right.

The first is that the market will fall from here. Fine. Markets do fall. Roughly one calendar year in four since 1928 has been negative, so this prediction is not absurd, it is merely a minority bet.

The second is the one nobody plans for: you have to know when to stop waiting.

Because a dip does not announce itself as a dip. On the day the market is down fifteen percent, it does not feel like an opportunity. It feels like the beginning of something worse, and it feels that way because it might be. The headlines on the day of the bottom are not optimistic. They are the worst headlines of the entire cycle. That is what produces the bottom.

So the person waiting for a dip must first correctly predict a fall, then find the courage to buy into the exact conditions that made everybody else sell. And they must do this without knowing whether the fall is over, using the same nervous system that was too anxious to buy when things were calm.

I have watched a great many people accomplish the first prediction. I have watched almost none of them accomplish the second. What actually happens is that the market falls, they feel briefly vindicated, they decide to wait for it to "stabilise," and then it recovers without them and they are now waiting for a dip from a higher level than the one they refused to buy at.

That is not a failure of nerve. It is the predictable output of a system that requires two correct decisions from a person who was uncomfortable making one.

THE BEST DAYS ARE HIDING INSIDE THE WORST ONES

Now the evidence, and it is unusually stark.

J.P. Morgan runs an analysis every year on what happens to a portfolio that steps out of the market briefly and misses the biggest single days. Take twenty years, 2003 to the end of 2022. Ten thousand dollars invested in the S&P 500 and left alone became $64,844.

The same ten thousand dollars, having missed just the ten best days out of roughly five thousand trading days, became $29,708.

Ten days. Out of twenty years. Less than half the money.

Push it further and it stops being funny. Missing the sixty best days over that period leaves you with $4,205, which is to say you turned ten thousand dollars into four thousand during two decades in which the market more than sixfold'd.

Expressed as annual returns over a slightly different window, July 2004 to July 2024, the pattern is the same: fully invested returns 10.5% a year, missing the ten best days drops you to 6.2%, missing twenty drops you to 3.6%, and missing thirty leaves 1.4%. At that point you have taken every ounce of equity risk and earned less than a guaranteed deposit.

Here is the detail that makes this fatal to market timing specifically, rather than merely alarming.

Seven of the ten best days occurred within fifteen days of the ten worst days.

Seven of the ten best days happened while the market was in bear territory. In 2015, the single best day of the year came two days after the single worst day of the year. In 2020, the second-best day arrived immediately after the second-worst.

The best days are not scattered pleasantly across calm periods. They live inside the wreckage. They are the market's violent recoil, and they happen precisely during the weeks when a sensible-sounding person has moved to cash to wait for things to settle down.

You cannot avoid the worst days and keep the best ones. They are the same weather.

In fairness, there is a real objection here, and I would rather give it to you than have you find it later and wonder what else I left out.

Critics point out, correctly, that the "ten best days" statistic is usually presented without its mirror image. If missing the best days is catastrophic, avoiding the worst days is spectacular. Bank of America data going back to 1930 suggests that missing the ten best days of each decade would have left an investor with a total return of 91%, against nearly fifteen thousand percent for holding through. But successfully dodging the ten worst days of each decade would have produced something like two and a half times the buy-and-hold result.

So yes: if you could reliably sidestep the crashes, you would do better than me. Enormously better.

The response is not that this is false. It is that the two are welded together. The best and worst days occupy the same fortnights, and any mechanism sensitive enough to get you out before the worst ones will still have you sitting in cash when the best ones fire, because they arrive within days of each other and nobody rings a bell in between. The critique proves the case it was written to attack. If the good days and the bad days were separable, somebody would have separated them by now, and the entire fund management industry we examined in the last chapter would look very different.

MEET BOB

There is an illustration I keep coming back to, published in 2014 by a writer named Ben Carlson, and it does more work than any chart I have ever seen. Bob is fictional. What happens to Bob is not.

Bob starts working in 1970, at twenty-two. He is a disciplined saver. He puts away two thousand dollars a year through the seventies, and raises it by two thousand each decade as his salary grows.

Bob has exactly one flaw as an investor, and it is the most common flaw there is: he can only bring himself to invest after the market has been going up for a while. He needs to feel safe before he acts.

So he invests four times in his entire life, and every single one of them is a disaster.

He puts his savings in at the end of 1972, immediately before the market falls roughly half.

He invests again in September 1987, days before Black Monday.

He invests again in 2000, at the summit of the technology bubble.

And he invests one final time in October 2007, just before the financial crisis takes another fifty percent.

Four decisions. Four peaks. Four crashes. If you set out deliberately to construct the worst possible timing record in modern financial history you would struggle to beat Bob, and Bob managed it by accident, using nothing more exotic than ordinary human caution.

He retires at the end of 2013 with more than a million dollars, from a total of $184,000 saved.

Bob did one thing right, and it was not a clever thing. He never sold. Not in 1974, not in 1987, not in 2002, not in 2009. He bought at the worst possible moments and then simply refused to leave.

I want to be careful about what this story does and does not prove. It does not prove that timing is irrelevant. Bob would have done considerably better buying steadily rather than in four terrified lumps.

Carlson built the illustration with a forty-one year runway, which is a luxury not everyone has, and Bob was invested entirely in one country's market, which is a bet in itself.

What it proves is narrower and more useful: bad timing, given enough time, is survivable. Not participating is not.

Bob's problem was never that he bought at the top. Bob's problem was the fourteen years he spent in a savings account between 1973 and 1987 waiting to feel safe, which is a form of timing too, and by far the more expensive one.

THE AWKWARD TRUTH ABOUT DOLLAR-COST AVERAGING

Now I have to complicate my own answer slightly, because the alternative is to be tidy and wrong.

You have probably been told that spreading your money out over time, buying a fixed amount at regular intervals, is the safest and smartest way to invest. It has a name, dollar-cost averaging, and it is what I am recommending in this chapter.

The awkward part is that on the pure mathematics, it is not the best strategy.

Vanguard ran the comparison across the US, UK and Australian markets going back to 1926. If you have a lump of money today and you must choose between investing all of it immediately or spreading it over the next twelve months, investing all of it immediately produced more wealth roughly two-thirds of the time, and by an average of a bit over two percent.

Later work, covering rolling one-year periods from 1976 to 2022, found the same shape: lump sum won somewhere between sixty-two and seventy-four percent of the time, depending on the market and the phase-in period.

The reason is not mysterious. The market goes up in about three years out of four. Money that is waiting to be invested is, on average, missing returns it could have been earning. Spreading your entry over a year is a quiet bet that prices will be lower later, and prices are usually not lower later.

So why am I telling you to buy in instalments?

Because the Vanguard study answers a question you do not have.

That study describes a person holding a large sum, deciding how fast to deploy it. Almost nobody reading this is that person. You have a job. Money arrives every two weeks, in a chunk, forever. You are not choosing between lump sum and instalments. Your income arrives in instalments, so your investing arrives in instalments. The debate is settled for you by the structure of employment.

And notice what your paycheque actually is, in this framework: every payday, you are lump-sum investing everything you have available. Which the data says is the right move. You are running the optimal strategy, involuntarily, forever.

The one time the question genuinely applies to you is if a large amount lands at once. An inheritance, a bonus, the proceeds of a sale. And there the honest answer has two layers.

The mathematics says invest it now. The mathematics is right about two-thirds of the time. But the mathematics does not have to live with the other third, and you do. If putting the whole sum in on a Tuesday and watching it fall twenty percent by Christmas would make you sell in a panic, then the theoretically inferior plan you can actually survive beats the optimal plan you will abandon.

That is not a failure of discipline.

That is discipline, correctly applied to the person you actually are rather than the one in the study.

WHY PAYDAY, SPECIFICALLY

So the trigger is your payday, and I want to explain why that particular trigger rather than a more thoughtful one. Because it removes the decision.

Every strategy that requires you to decide when to buy will eventually meet a week when you feel clever, or frightened, or busy, and the decision will go badly. A strategy that fires automatically on the day you are paid never meets that week at all. You are not exercising judgement. You are removing the opportunity to exercise judgement, which is a different and much more reliable thing.

Set it up once. Money leaves your account on the day it arrives, buys the thing you chose in Chapter One, and you never touch it. Most brokerages and banks will do this automatically. The entire apparatus takes twenty minutes to build and then runs for three decades.

I have a small confession about this. The reason I invest automatically is not that I am disciplined. It is that I have direct evidence I am not. My own record from 2019 is in the foreword of this book, and it consists of a man who could not leave a position alone for a fortnight. Automation is not a virtue I possess. It is a fence I built around a habit I could not fix.

If you are the sort of person who genuinely can look at a screen full of red and do nothing, then you do not need the fence, and you may buy manually with my blessing.

I have met perhaps three such people. Two of them were lying.

But the Market Is at an All-Time High

This objection deserves its own section, because it is the one that stops more people than any other, and because it sounds like caution rather than error.

Here is the thing about all-time highs. In a market that trends upward over decades, all-time highs are not a warning sign. They are the normal condition. A rising index spends an enormous amount of its life at or near a record, because that is what rising means. Waiting for the market not to be near a high is waiting for the market to have stopped doing the thing you are buying it for.

Ask yourself what the alternative sounds like when you say it out loud. I will invest once the market has been performing badly for a while. That is a rule that guarantees you buy only during periods of fear, which is exactly the period in which you will feel least able to buy. Bob's rule, in reverse, with the same result.

And notice the trap in the logic. If the market falls after

you invest, you were right to be worried. If it rises, you were right to be worried and you missed it, and now the high is higher. The rule has no exit. There is no future price at which a person who is scared of highs becomes comfortable, because the fear was never about the price.

WHAT THIS WILL COST YOU

I am not going to pretend this is free, because a promise without a cost attached is a sales pitch.

Buying on a schedule means you will buy at peaks. Repeatedly. Some of your purchases will be at the worst prices of the decade, and you will know it within months, and it will feel exactly as bad as you imagine.

You will also buy at the bottoms. You will not notice those, because nothing dramatic happens when you accidentally do something right, and by the time the bottom is visible as a bottom you will have forgotten which fortnight it was.

That asymmetry is worth naming. The bad purchases announce themselves loudly and the good ones stay silent, so your memory of this strategy will always be worse than its results.

Plan for that now. In ten years, when you feel like your timing has been unlucky, remember that you are recalling a biased sample.

The other cost is the one people underestimate. You are giving up the story. There is no version of this where you get to tell someone at a dinner party that you called the bottom in March. You have chosen a method that works and cannot be bragged about, and for some people that trade is genuinely difficult.

THE SMALL PRINT

Two practical notes, and then we are done.

Frequency matters less than you think. Weekly, fortnightly, monthly, it makes very little difference over thirty years. Match it to your pay cycle and stop optimising. The difference between monthly and weekly investing is a rounding error next to the difference between investing and not.

Costs matter more than you think. If your platform charges a commission on every purchase, buying weekly with a small amount can hand a meaningful slice of your money to the broker.

Check what a trade costs you. If it is not free, buy monthly instead. This is one of the very few places in this book where the specific mechanics can actually change the outcome.

Where That Leaves Us

Two questions answered.

You know what to buy: the whole market, at low cost, in something you can describe in one sentence.

You know when: now, and on every payday afterwards, automatically, without ever again asking whether the moment is right.

Notice that both answers have the same shape. Both replaced a judgement with a rule. Both took a decision that was being made repeatedly, badly, under emotional pressure, and made it once, in advance, in a calm room.
That is not a coincidence. It is the method of this entire book.

And it brings us to the third question, which is the one that quietly determines whether you will still be following any of this in five years.

THE GAP

QUESTION NUMBER 3

HOW MUCH TO BUY?

"ONLY THOSE WHO WILL BE SELLERS OF EQUITIES IN THE NEAR FUTURE SHOULD BE HAPPY AT SEEING STOCKS RISE."

WARREN BUFFETT, 1997

THE WOMAN WITH THE COFFEE

She buys the same coffee every week. Same brand, same shelf, same size, for about nine years now.

One Saturday she turns into the aisle and it is thirty percent off. Not a substitute, not a clearance item near its date. The exact bag she was going to buy anyway, marked down for no reason she needs to investigate.

So she takes four. She feels the specific satisfaction of a person who has beaten the system slightly, and she mentions it to her husband when she gets home, and if you asked her she would tell you it was a good day.

That evening she opens the app on her phone to check her investments, because she has heard the market has had a bad week.

Her portfolio, which is one stock, is down thirty percent. She does not sleep well. She spends most of Sunday deciding whether to sell it on Monday.

Same person. Same day. Same number.

In the morning, thirty percent off was a reason to buy four. By the evening, thirty percent off was a reason to get out.

I have watched this happen to intelligent people my entire adult life, and I have done it myself, and it took me an embarrassingly long time to notice that the two reactions cannot both be correct.

Warren Buffett noticed it in 1997, and put it more precisely than I can. He asked his shareholders a short quiz. If you plan to eat hamburgers for the rest of your life and you do not raise cattle, should you want beef to be cheaper or more expensive? If you will buy a car occasionally and you do not manufacture cars, which way should you want car prices to move?

The questions answer themselves. Then he asked the one that does not.

If you expect to be a net saver over the next five years, should you hope for a higher stock market or a lower one?

Most people get it wrong. They are going to be buying the

stocks for decades, and they cheer when the price of the thing they are about to buy goes up, and they despair when it goes on sale. As Buffett put it, the only people who should be pleased by rising prices are the ones about to sell.

You are not about to sell. You just read two chapters explaining that you will be buying every payday for next several years.

Which means a falling market is not something happening to you. It is a sale on everything you have not bought yet. Hold onto that, because this chapter is where it becomes practical.

The Answer:

AS MUCH AS YOU CAN LEAVE COMPLETELY ALONE. NOT ONE DOLLAR MORE.

That is the answer, and it is deliberately not a formula.

You will find books that give you a formula. Subtract your age from a hundred, put that percentage in equities. It is tidy, it is memorable, and it is guessing dressed up as mathematics, because it knows nothing about your job security, your obligations, your temperament, or what you did the last time you watched a number fall.

The right amount is a personal number, but it is not an arbitrary one. There is a method for finding it, and this chapter is that method.

Notice, though, what the answer is not about. It is not about how much you can afford. Almost everyone can afford to invest more than they do. The binding constraint is not your income. It is the point at which the volatility starts making decisions for you.

Invest more than that, and you will sell at the bottom. Everything in this book fails at that moment. So the amount is not a financial optimisation. It is a psychological one, and the right number is the largest one you will not flinch at.

TWO GATES BEFORE ANY OF THIS

Before a single dollar goes into the market, two things have to be true. I will keep this brief, because both are subjects for other books, and probably other authors.

One: six months of expenses, in cash, untouched.

Not three, not a vague sense that you would manage. Six months of what it actually costs you to live, sitting in a savings account earning whatever you can get, doing nothing.

This is not investment money that you happen to be storing badly. It is a completely different instrument with a completely different job. Its job is to make sure that when the car dies in the same month the contract ends, you solve the problem with cash instead of by selling your investments at whatever price the market happens to be offering that Tuesday.

Every catastrophic investing story I have heard has this at its centre. Not a bad stock. A forced sale. The market fell, and something in life went wrong at the same time, and the person had no choice, and a temporary loss became a permanent one at the worst possible moment.

If you do not have six months saved, you are not behind on investing. You are simply at an earlier stage of the same project. Fill the fund first. It is not exciting and nobody posts about it.

Two: expensive debt, gone.

If you are carrying a balance at nineteen or twenty percent, no investment discussed in this book competes with paying it off.

A guaranteed nineteen percent return, which is what clearing that debt is, beats an uncertain ten percent every time, in every market, forever.

There is no cleverness required here and no counter-argument worth your time.

Mortgages and low-rate student loans are a genuinely different conversation, and reasonable people disagree. High-interest consumer debt is not a conversation at all.

Both gates closed? Good.

Now we can talk about *the number*.

FINDING YOUR NUMBER

Here is the exercise. It takes about a minute.

Picture the total amount you expect to have invested. Not this month's contribution. The whole thing, a year or two from now, once you have been at it a while.

Got a number? Good.

Now imagine opening the app one morning and finding that number has fallen by forty percent.

Fifty thousand has become thirty thousand. Ten thousand has become six thousand. Whatever your number was, take four dollars out of every ten and look at what is left.

Sit with the smaller figure for a moment, because it is not a thought experiment. It is a Tuesday that is coming.

Falls of that size are not rare and they are not ancient history. In 2008 the American market fell thirty-eight percent in a single calendar year. Between 2000 and 2002 it lost about half its value. From late 2007 to early 2009 it lost more than half. Anyone reading this who was an adult in either period watched it happen.

Invest for thirty years and you will almost certainly see something in that range at least once, and quite possibly twice.

So, looking at the smaller number, answer one question honestly.

Not "*would I be upset?*" Of course you would be upset. I would be upset.

The question is: *Would I still put money in the following month?*

If yes, the amount is fine. Go ahead.

If no, the amount is too big. And no amount of further reading about the merits of index investing will fix that, because the problem was never your understanding. It is your nervous system, and your nervous system does not read.

So bring the number down until the answer is yes. Invest that. Then raise it later, after you have lived through something ugly and discovered you were sturdier than you expected.

Almost everybody is. Nobody knows it in advance. Start where you actually are, not where you would like to be.

WHY PEOPLE GET THIS WRONG IN BOTH DIRECTIONS

There are two failure modes here and they look nothing alike.

Too much. This one is obvious and it is the one everybody warns you about. Money goes into the market that was needed for something, or that the person could not psychologically carry, and it comes out again at the worst possible time. The market did not fail them. The sizing did.

Too little. This one is quieter and it costs far more people far more money, and almost nobody warns you about it, because it never produces a dramatic story.

The too-little investor puts in an amount so small that it cannot affect their life, and then congratulates themselves on being sensible. Fifty dollars a month, thirty years, while sixty thousand sits in a savings account earning almost nothing because that feels safe.

Fifty dollars a month for thirty years at ten percent gets you somewhere around a hundred thousand dollars. That is a genuinely good outcome for fifty dollars a month. But the sixty thousand sitting still, at the same rate over the same period, would have become well over a million.

The person who invested too little did not lose money. They will never see a red number that upsets them.

They simply arrive at sixty-five having quietly declined an outcome that was available to them, and they will never know it happened, because nothing happened.

That is the whole tragedy of the second failure mode. It is invisible from the inside.

I have known several people in this category. Every one of them describes themselves as cautious.

None of them has ever calculated what the caution cost.

What a Solid Portfolio Actually Looks Like

Now the part people usually mean when they ask about allocation. How many things should you own, and in what proportions?

The short answer is going to disappoint you: fewer things than you think, in simpler proportions than you expect.

Here is the principle underneath it. Diversification is not a measure of how many products you own. It is a measure of how many genuinely different outcomes you are exposed to. Those are not the same, and the gap between them is where most amateur portfolios go wrong.

Somebody owns a global fund, a US fund, a technology fund, and three individual technology companies. They have six positions. They will tell you they are diversified. In reality, all six are heavily exposed to the same twenty or thirty enormous companies, so when those companies have a bad year, every single line on their statement is red simultaneously, and they cannot work out why, because the whole point of owning six things was that this should not happen.

That is not a portfolio. That is one bet, purchased six times, at six sets of fees.

The test I would use. Can you say in one sentence what you own and why each piece is there? If explaining your portfolio takes more than a sentence, or if any piece exists because it did well recently, that piece is probably not diversification. It is enthusiasm with a ticker symbol.

For most people reading this, the honest answer is that a single broad global equity fund does the entire job. One product, thousands of companies, dozens of countries, rebalancing itself as the world changes, at a cost of a fraction of a percent. There is no prize for complexity. Nobody is grading your portfolio on how interesting it is.

If you want a second holding, have a reason that is not performance. "I want more exposure to my own country because my pension and my house and my job are all denominated in this currency" is a reason. "It has done well lately" is not a reason, it is a description of the past.

On individual companies: If you want to own some, own some. I am not going to pretend the urge does not exist, and forbidding it usually produces a person who does it secretly and badly. But cap it.

Pick a number, five percent of your portfolio or ten at the outside, decide it now while you are calm, and never let it grow beyond that through additional purchases.

And understand what you are buying, which is entertainment with a positive expected cost. The evidence in the first chapter of this book was not ambiguous about the odds.

If holding a few companies keeps you engaged enough to stay invested for thirty years, that is a real benefit and it may well be worth the fee.

Just call it what it is.

THE OPPORTUNITY FUND

Now the part of my own approach that I have argued about with myself the most, and I am going to give you both sides, including the one that disagrees with me.

I keep a slice of my portfolio, somewhere between five and ten percent, in cash. Not the emergency fund, which is separate and untouchable. This is inside the investment side of the ledger. I think of it as an opportunity fund.

Its job is this. When the market falls hard, and everything I already wanted to own is suddenly available for meaningfully less, I have something to buy with. Not because I predicted the fall. Because falls happen, on a schedule nobody publishes, and I would rather meet one with money in my hand than with regret.

To be precise about what I am not doing, since Chapter Two was quite firm on this: I am not sitting on money that should be invested, waiting for a better price. If I have a thousand dollars to put to work this month, nine hundred goes in immediately. The hundred is not being withheld from the market. It is a standing position, permanently sized, that I refill on subsequent paydays after I use it.

Now the argument against, which is strong and which you deserve to hear.

The research on this is not kind. AQR examined exactly this behaviour, comparing investors who deploy cash immediately against those who hold some back for dips, and found the dip-waiters ended up with about nineteen percent less wealth. Across nearly two hundred variations of the strategy tested over sixty years, only eight percent showed any statistically significant outperformance. A separate study published in European Financial Management in 2024 found no reliable advantage either.

The reason is the one Chapter Two gave. Cash that is waiting is cash that is not compounding, and the market rises in roughly three years out of four, so the waiting usually costs more than the discount saves.

I know this. I do it anyway, and I want to be honest about why, because the reason is not that I think the researchers are wrong.

I hold the opportunity fund because of what it does to me during a crash, not what it does to my returns.

When the market falls thirty percent, a person with dry powder experiences an opportunity. A person without it experiences only loss. Those are the same event and completely different weeks, and I know which version of me stays invested. The fund costs me somewhere between half a percent and one percent a year in expected return, and it buys something I consider worth more than that: it makes bad markets feel like something I am participating in rather than something being done to me.

That is a trade, and it is a defensible one, but it is a trade. Anyone who tells you dry powder is free money is selling something.

So here is my honest instruction. If you are the sort of person who will hold steady through a crash without it, do not bother. Invest everything, immediately, always, and you will very likely finish with more.

If you suspect you are not that person, and most people are not, then five to ten percent held aside is a reasonable price to pay for staying in the game. Just size it deliberately, name it, and never let it creep upwards, because an opportunity fund that grows to thirty percent is not an opportunity fund. It is fear with a job title.

WHEN IT FALLS

One last thing about amounts, and it is the point the coffee story was really for.

If you have sized this correctly, a falling market should produce a very specific feeling in you, and it is not bravery. It is not even calm.

It should feel like the coffee aisle.

Everything you have spent months buying at full price is now available for less, and you have thirty years of purchases ahead of you, and the only people who should be upset about this are the ones planning to sell soon. You are not one of them. You said so in Chapter One.

If a falling market does not feel remotely like a sale, that is not a character flaw. It is information. It means the amount is too large, or the horizon is too short, or something in your life is closer than you admitted when you did the arithmetic. Go back to the multiplication and be more honest the second time.

The size is right when the fall is interesting rather than frightening.

That is the whole of the third question. Enough that it matters, never so much that it decides for you, held in something simple enough to explain in a sentence, with a little kept back if that is what keeps you steady.

Which leaves one question, and it is the one you have been waiting for since the foreword.

When to sell.

THE GAP

QUESTION NUMBER 4

–

WHEN TO SELL?

"IT NEVER WAS MY THINKING THAT MADE THE BIG MONEY FOR ME. IT ALWAYS WAS MY SITTING."

JESSE LIVERMORE

Livermore was the most famous speculator of his generation. He made and lost several fortunes, shorted the crash of 1929, and died broke in 1940.

I have chosen him deliberately. That line is not the wisdom of a patient man. It is the confession of a man who could not stop moving, admitting at the height of his powers that every dollar he ever kept came from the periods when he did nothing.

The Answer:

NEVER.

That is the answer to the fourth question, and I have been building toward it since the foreword.

Now, before you close the book and write a review about how that cannot possibly be right, stay with me a little longer. Because "never" is doing something more precise than it looks, and the precision is the whole point. And because the answer is not really about selling at all. It is about what you are holding.

If you answered the first three questions properly, you are sitting on something you have no reason to part with. Not something you must grimly refuse to part with. Something genuinely worth keeping, in every market, in every mood, for the rest of your life. Selling it would be an act against your own interest, and the reason you will not do it is not restraint. It is that there is nothing better to do with the money.

If you answered the first three questions badly, no amount of instruction in this chapter will save you, because you will be trying to hold on to something you were right to doubt. Let me first tell you what "never" does not mean.

THREE THINGS THAT LOOK LIKE SELLING AND ARE NOT

ONE: SPENDING THE MONEY.

You did not invest in order to have an investment. You invested in order to have a life that the money pays for. Retirement, a house, a child's education, a decade of not going to work.

The day you begin drawing on this to live is not the day the plan failed. It is the day the plan worked. The whole apparatus existed to produce that morning.

So when I say never sell, I am not asking you to die holding a large portfolio and a strong sense of discipline. I am talking about the years in which you are building. Selling as an act of consumption, on a schedule you planned years in advance, is not selling in the sense this chapter means. It is harvesting.

The distinction is simple and it holds all the way through: selling to fund your life is the point. Selling to fix a feeling is the failure.

TWO: HOUSEKEEPING.

Sometimes you will own something slightly wrong. Two funds that turn out to hold nearly the same companies. A holding you bought before you understood what you were doing. A product with a fee that a cheaper equivalent has since undercut.

Consolidating those is not exiting the market. The money never leaves. You sell one thing on Tuesday morning and own the equivalent thing by Tuesday afternoon, with lower costs or a simpler statement. Your exposure to the world's businesses does not change by a single day.

I may do exactly this myself at some point, tidying two overlapping holdings into one. That is not a betrayal of anything in this chapter. It is the equivalent of moving your savings to a bank paying a better rate. Nobody would call that abandoning saving.

THREE: REBALANCING.

If you have deliberately chosen proportions, and time has pushed them out of shape, restoring them is maintenance rather than judgement. It fires on a number you set in advance, not on a view about what happens next.

The test that separates all three of these from the thing this chapter forbids is a single question: did the decision come from your plan, or from the price?

Housekeeping, harvesting, and rebalancing come from the plan. They would have happened at any price.

WHAT "NEVER" ACTUALLY FORBIDS

So here is the rule in its exact form.

Never sell because of what the price did, or because of how the price made you feel.

That is it. That is the entire prohibition, and once you see it clearly you notice something strange about it: almost every sale that ever destroyed anybody's wealth falls inside it.

They sold because it fell and they were frightened.

They sold because it rose and they wanted to lock in the win.

They sold because it had gone sideways for two years and they were bored, which is the most underrated reason people wreck a portfolio.

They sold because someone on television used the word "correction" in a tone they did not like.

Notice that in every one of those cases the world's businesses continued doing exactly what they had been doing the day before. Nothing changed about the thousands of companies inside the fund. Something changed on a screen, and something changed inside a person, and those two things had a conversation, and the person lost.

THE COST OF THAT CONVERSATION

We can measure this, and the measurement is one of the more sobering numbers in retail finance.

Morningstar publishes a study each year called Mind the Gap. It does something simple. It compares what funds returned to what the people who owned those funds actually earned, and the difference between the two is entirely explained by when investors chose to put money in and take it out.

In the 2025 edition, covering the decade to the end of 2024, the funds returned 8.2 percent a year. The people who owned them earned 7.0 percent. A gap of 1.2 percentage points every year, which Morningstar notes is around fifteen percent of everything those funds produced over the period. And it is not a one-off. The same gap appears in the studies ending in 2020, 2021, 2022 and 2023.

The pattern within the data is the one that should get your attention. The most volatile funds produced the widest gaps, around 1.8 percentage points. Sector funds, the exciting ones, trailed by 1.5. And the simple all-in-one allocation funds, the boring diversified products that give an owner almost nothing to react to, had a gap of 0.1.

Not zero because their owners were more disciplined. Near zero because there was nothing to do. The design of the product removed the opportunity to sabotage it.

In fairness, this study has been challenged, and since I have made a point of showing you the other side elsewhere in this book, I will do it here too. A 2026 paper by Fulkerson, Jordan, Riley and Yan argued that the return gap is not mostly caused by bad timing at all, and that when you isolate timing specifically, the cost is closer to 0.10 percent a year. Some of what looks like investor error is really the arithmetic of money arriving in funds at different times.

I think that critique is worth knowing and I do not think it rescues anybody. Even at the low estimate, the direction is the same, and the pattern that volatile funds produce bigger gaps than boring ones does not go away. But you should know the debate exists.

Take the higher figure for a moment, because the compounding makes the point. A hundred thousand dollars growing at ten percent for twenty years becomes about $673,000. The same hundred thousand, giving up 1.2 percent a year, becomes about $540,000.

Nearly twenty percent of the outcome, gone, without a single bad investment being chosen. Every product was fine. The owner just kept touching it.

THE TWO COSTS NOBODY COUNTS

Beyond the behaviour, selling carries two mechanical costs that people consistently forget.
Tax. In a taxable account, selling an appreciated holding triggers a bill. Money that would have kept compounding for another thirty years instead goes to a government this April. Not eventually. Now, and permanently, along with every dollar it would have earned.

This is the quiet argument for never selling that has nothing to do with psychology. An investor who holds for forty years defers that tax for forty years, and the deferred amount compounds the entire time on their behalf. An investor who trades in and out pays it repeatedly, resetting the clock each time. Over a lifetime the difference is enormous and it requires no skill whatsoever to capture. You simply do nothing, and the tax code rewards you for it.

Retirement accounts change these mechanics, and the rules differ by country, so this is one of the few places in this book where you genuinely should ask somebody who knows your situation.

Re-entry. The second cost is the one people never plan for. Selling is one decision. Getting back in is another, and it is far harder, because you will be trying to buy at a price you already refused once.

If you sold at a 30 percent decline, you now need to buy back either lower, which requires the very forecast you could not make in Chapter Two, or higher, which requires admitting you were wrong and paying a premium for the privilege. Most people cannot do either, so they wait. And waiting, as we established, is a position with a cost attached.

This is how a temporary decline becomes a permanent one. Not through the fall. Through the sale, and the paralysis afterwards.

THE ONLY REASON THAT COUNTS

There is one legitimate reason to exit an investment, and it is worth stating clearly so that ”never” does not become a superstition.

Sell when the reason you bought it has stopped being true.

If the facts change, your mind should change. That is not weakness, it is the entire basis of thinking honestly.

Now apply that test to what you actually own.

If you own a single company, this happens regularly. Businesses lose their advantage, get disrupted, are caught doing something appalling, or simply stop being good at the thing that made them worth owning. A company's reason for existing can genuinely expire, and if you own companies you have to monitor for it, which is one more argument for the answer we reached in Chapter One.

But you do not own a company. You own an index fund holding thousands of businesses across dozens of countries, weighted by size, which replaces its own constituents automatically as the world changes.

So what would have to happen for your reason to stop being true?

Not a recession. Recessions are inside the historical record that produced the return.

Not a crash. Also inside the record.

Not a company failing. The fund is designed to drop failures and add their replacements without asking you.

Not a country declining. If one market shrinks and another grows, a global fund reweights toward the growth. That is what "global" means. It survived the relative decline of Britain and it survived the relative decline of Japan, and it did so without anyone needing to make a call. The honest answer is that for a broadly diversified fund to lose its reason for existing, human enterprise as a whole would have to stop creating value. That is not an investing scenario. That is a scenario in which your portfolio is not the pressing issue.

And that is the trick of the fourth question. Not that selling is forbidden by an act of will. That when you own the right thing, the condition that would justify selling stops being reachable.

This is why I keep returning to the first three questions rather than to your character. A portfolio built on the right answers is not a burden you carry. It is an asset with no expiry date, no maintenance schedule, and no news cycle attached to it. There is no version of the future in which parting with it is the intelligent move, so you never have to develop the willpower not to.

NOW, THE REVEAL

In the foreword I told you one of these four questions would disappear before the end, and that you would probably be surprised by which one.

You guessed this one. Of course you did. It is called When to Sell and you were three chapters into a book that clearly had opinions.

You guessed right, and for the wrong reason.

Almost everyone assumes the fourth question dissolves because I am going to demand extraordinary discipline. That "never sell" is a feat of willpower, a thing you grit your teeth through while your holdings fall and your hands shake.

It is not. That version fails, and it fails for exactly the reason Chapter One warned about: a rule you have to force yourself to obey is a rule you will abandon on the morning it matters.

Here is what actually happens.

The fourth question was never a question. It was a consequence.

Go back through what you have already decided.

You bought something you do not need to monitor, so no news can arrive that changes your view of it. There is nothing to react to, because you own everything, so a bad story about any one company is a story about roughly nothing.

You buy on a schedule, automatically, regardless of price, so a fall does not require a decision from you. Your next purchase happens on payday whether the market is euphoric or on fire.

And you sized it so that a forty percent decline leaves you interested rather than frightened, with money you will not need for decades and a buffer that means no emergency can force your hand.

Now tell me what triggers a sale.

The price fell? You have no mechanism that responds to price, and the fall makes your next purchase cheaper, which you already decided was good news in Chapter Three. The price rose? Selling would mean owning less of the thing you spent three chapters concluding you wanted. You need the money? You do not, because you sized it so you would not. The reason expired? It cannot, for the reasons we just covered.

There is no path. Not because you are strong. Because you built something with no exit door in it, back when you were calm and reading a book, rather than at eleven at night with a red screen in your hand.

Answer the first three questions properly and your portfolio is gold. Not gold as in the metal, which does nothing. Gold as in the thing nobody sensible hands over, at any price, for any reason, because there is nothing on offer that they would rather have.

That is what I meant in the foreword when I said the question would dissolve rather than be answered. The first three questions did not lead up to the fourth. They ate it.
You do not need a selling strategy. A selling strategy is what people need when the first three answers were wrong.

THE WOMAN ON THE BIKE

I want to end where this book started.

There is a woman in my gym, on a bike, who has been losing money for eleven years while feeling good about it. She was never going to be rescued by a better fund. Her problem was not the product she owned. It was that nobody ever put four questions in front of her in a calm room and showed her what a good answer looked like, so she outsourced all four to somebody with an incentive, and then stopped thinking about it, and eleven years went by.

And there is a younger version of me, in 2019, doing the opposite thing and arriving at the same place. Reading annual reports at midnight, switching positions, working extremely hard at all four questions and answering every one of them badly, and ending up level with a form you sign at a bank counter.

Between the two of them sits the whole of this book. She never asked the questions. I asked them constantly and answered them with my nervous system. Neither of us got anywhere, and both of us thought we were doing fine, and that is the part that should frighten you, because feeling fine is not evidence of anything at all.

The gap is not between people who are clever and people who are not. It is between people who decided in advance and people who decide in the moment. That is all it has ever been.

What Happens Now

You are going to close this book, and within a month you will be tested, because the market is always doing something and somebody is always explaining it loudly.

Some of it you will handle easily. What will actually get you is smaller and more boring than a crash. A colleague with a stock that tripled. A stretch of two flat years where the whole thing seems pointless. A headline using a word you find alarming. An account balance that has gone sideways long enough for you to start wondering whether you should be doing something.

The urge, when it arrives, will not feel like panic. It will feel like initiative.

When it does, I would ask you to do one thing, and it is the reason this book has four chapters instead of forty.

Ask which of the four questions you are actually being asked.

Should I buy this thing my colleague bought? That is question one, and you answered it.

Should I wait for a better moment? That is question two, and you answered it.

Should I put more in, or less? That is question three, and you answered it, and you can revisit it deliberately in a calm month if your life has changed.

Should I get out? That is question four, and it does not exist. It never did.

It never did because the first three questions, answered honestly, leave you owning something you would be mad to give up. That is the whole of it. Get those three right and the fourth never comes for you. Get them wrong and it will come for you constantly, in every falling market, for as long as you own the wrong thing.

Four questions. Answered once, properly, in a quiet room, by a version of you who was not frightened.

That is the entire method. It is not popularly considered as *clever*, and it will not make an interesting story at a dinner party, but *it will very likely make you very wealthy.*

One Last Thing

I have been carrying these four questions around for six years now, and I want to tell you what they are actually for.

They are not for making money. Money is the byproduct.

They are for getting your attention back.

Before I understood any of this, investing occupied a genuinely absurd amount of my head. I checked prices in meetings. I read commentary I did not understand written by people who did not know me. I had opinions about interest rates. I lay awake, on more than one occasion, over a company whose products I had never used and whose employees would not have recognised my name.

I did not become wealthy during those years. I did not even become well informed. I simply spent a portion of my one life on a screen, in exchange for a return I could have matched by signing a form.

What the four questions gave me was not a better portfolio. It was Sunday evenings.

That is what I would like you to take from this book, if you take anything.

Not that index funds are good, though they are. Not that fees compound against you, though they do. But that this whole subject, which an entire industry has spent decades making complicated and urgent and frightening, can be settled in an afternoon and then left alone for forty years.

You are not supposed to spend your life managing money. You are supposed to spend your life.

Four questions. Answered once, in a quiet room, by a version of you who was not frightened. And then a very long stretch of not thinking about any of it, while the thing you built quietly does what it was always going to do.

Thank you for reading. Go and live your life.

A LETTER TO THE READER

Thank you for reading this one. I would like to tell you something I have not said anywhere else in the book.

The Gap is the last book I intend to write about money.

Not because I have run out of interest, but because I have run out of things I am certain about. Three books ago I set out to explain what I wished somebody had explained to me at twenty-six, and it turned out to take exactly three: one about how to measure, one about who to be sceptical of, and this one about what to actually do. I do not have a fourth, and I would rather stop here than pad the shelf.

Which makes this the end of a project I have been living inside for several years, and I find I am not sad about it. The whole argument of these books is that this subject should take up less of your life, not more.

It seems only fair that I take my own advice.

If this one was useful, the other two are *The Game of Percentage*, which is about reading your own results honestly, and *The Effortless Investor*, which is about the industry that would prefer you did not.

You can find them by searching for it by the title or by my name on Amazon, Goodreads, or Google.

Two small requests, and then I will let you go.

If you have a few minutes, please leave a review on Amazon or Goodreads. Not a favour to me, though it is that. Reviews are the only reason a book like this reaches anyone at all, and a paragraph from you does more for it than anything I could pay for. Tell people what you disagreed with, too. That is more useful to the next reader than praise.

And if the book prompted you to actually change something, I would like to hear about it. Not a compliment. The change. That is the only measure of whether any of this worked.

You can also find me on Social media platforms such as Instagram @Author_Sriram_Saravanan, and on LinkedIn at www.linkedin.com/in/SriramSaravanan.

Now go and set up the transfer, if you have not already.

Sincerely,

Sriram Saravanan

A Note on Sources

I have kept citations out of the body of this book, because footnotes on the page tend to make people read more slowly and enjoy it less. But every figure in these pages came from somewhere, and you are entitled to check my work. Here is where each of them came from, in the order they appear.

Where I have summarised a study, I would encourage you to read the original. Most are freely available, and several are more interesting than my summary of them.

Foreword

Canadian inflation, 2022. Statistics Canada, Consumer Price Index, annual review 2022. Inflation averaged 6.8 percent for the year, the largest annual increase since 1982, peaking at 8.1 percent in June.

statcan.gc.ca

Indian fixed deposit rates. Rates of around 7 to 8 percent on one-year deposits at private banks were typical during the period described.

Question One: What to Buy

The "sharpen the axe" quotation. The line commonly attributed to Abraham Lincoln has no basis. Quote Investigator traced it and found no evidence Lincoln said anything of the kind; the earliest matching version appeared in 1956, in a volume on agricultural education, credited to an anonymous woodsman.

Reported in Philadelphia Magazine, 7 April 2016, citing Quote Investigator.

Josiah Strong, The Times and Young Men (New York, 1901). The verifiable version of the same idea.

Canadian savings account rates. Comparison of ongoing rates across major and online banks. The average ongoing rate across the accounts surveyed was under 1 percent, with standard savings accounts at the largest banks paying as little as 0.01 to 0.20 percent, while several CDIC-insured online banks paid multiples of that.

Canadian GIC rates. As of July 2026, the highest one-year GIC rate available in Canada was 3.60 percent, and the highest five-year rate 4.05 percent. The Bank of Canada overnight rate stood at 2.25 percent.

ratehub.ca/gics/best-gic-rates

Canadian fund fees. Asset-weighted average management expense ratios: 0.32 percent for long-term Canada-listed ETFs, 0.89 percent for fee-based mutual fund series, and 1.47 percent across all mutual fund series. The MER is deducted automatically and does not appear as a line item on investor statements.

Hendrik Bessembinder, "Do Stocks Outperform Treasury Bills?" Journal of Financial Economics, vol. 129, no. 3 (2018), pp. 440–457.

The source of the central argument in this chapter. Bessembinder examined every common stock in the CRSP database from 1926 onward and found that four out of every seven had lifetime buy-and-hold returns below one-month Treasury bills; that the best-performing 4 percent of listed companies (1,092 firms) account for the entire net gain of the US stock market over the period; that roughly 90 companies, slightly more than one third of one percent of all listings, produced more than half of all wealth creation; and that in bootstrap simulations a single randomly chosen stock underperformed the value-weighted market in 96 percent of cases and underperformed one-month Treasury bills in 73 percent.

papers.ssrn.com/sol3/papers.cfm?abstract_id=2900447

Bessembinder's 2023 extension, covering 1926 to 2022, found that 58.6 percent of the 28,114 US stocks ever listed reduced rather than increased shareholder wealth, and that 72 firms explain half of all net wealth creation.

SPIVA (S&P Indices Versus Active) Scorecard. Published by S&P Dow Jones Indices since 2002.

In 2025, 79 percent of active large-cap US equity funds underperformed the S&P 500, the fourth-worst showing for active management in the scorecard's 25-year history. Over fifteen years, roughly 90 percent of large-cap funds underperformed; over twenty years, approximately 92 percent. At the fifteen-year horizon there was no category in which a majority of active managers outperformed. The companion Persistence Scorecard found that among funds finishing in the top half in 2021, very few remained in the top half over the following four years, with large-cap results worse than random chance would predict.

spglobal.com/spdji/en/research-insights/spiva/

The challenge to SPIVA. A 2026 study sponsored by the Investment Adviser Association's Active Managers Council argued that SPIVA's methodology understates active fund performance. Readers should be aware both that the objection exists and that it was funded by the parties being measured.

S&P 500 long-run returns. Approximately 10 percent per year nominal since 1928 with dividends reinvested, and approximately 6.9 percent after inflation. Decade variation is substantial: the 1950s returned about 19.5 percent annually, the 2000s lost 0.9 percent annually (a real loss of 3.4 percent), and the 1970s returned about 5.9 percent nominal while losing purchasing power. Notable single-year declines include 1931 (down 47.1 percent), 1937 (down 38.6 percent), 2008 (down 38.5 percent), 1974 (down 29.7 percent), and 2022 (down 19.4 percent).

Underlying data from Robert Shiller, Yale University, and MacroTrends.

Question Two: When to Buy

"Time in the market beats timing the market." No reliable attribution exists. The line circulates credited to several well-known investors, none of whom appear to have originated it.

Vanguard, "Dollar-cost averaging just means taking risk later" (Vanguard Research, 2012).

Comparing immediate lump-sum investment against twelve-month dollar-cost averaging across US, UK and Australian markets, lump-sum investing produced higher wealth roughly two-thirds of the time, by an average of about 2.3 percent. Later Vanguard work covering rolling one-year periods from 1976 to 2022 found lump sum won between 61.6 and 73.7 percent of the time.

Morgan Stanley reached a similar conclusion across more than a thousand overlapping seven-year periods, finding lump-sum investing produced higher annualised returns in roughly two-thirds of cases.

J.P. Morgan Asset Management, "cost of missing the best days" analysis.

A $10,000 investment in the S&P 500 from 1 January 2003 to 30 December 2022 grew to $64,844 if left alone; to $29,708 if the ten best days were missed; and to $4,205 if the sixty best days were missed. Measured as annualised returns from July 2004 to July 2024: 10.5 percent fully invested, 6.2 percent missing the ten best days, 3.6 percent missing twenty, and 1.4 percent missing thirty. Seven of the ten best days occurred within fifteen days of the ten worst, and seven occurred while the market was in bear territory.

www.jpmorgan.com

The counter-argument. Lance Roberts and others have noted that the "best days" statistic is typically presented without its mirror image, and that successfully avoiding the ten worst days of each decade would have produced roughly two and a half times the buy-and-hold result. Bank of America data from 1930 onward supports the arithmetic. The objection is sound and is addressed in the chapter.

Ben Carlson, "What if You Only Invested at Market Peaks?" A Wealth of Common Sense, February 2014.

The origin of "Bob, the world's worst market timer." Bob is a fictional illustration: a saver who invests only four times, at the market peaks of 1972, 1987, 2000 and 2007, and never sells. Carlson's methodology uses the S&P 500 less a 0.20 percent expense ratio to 1977 and actual Vanguard 500 Index Fund results thereafter.

awealthofcommonsense.com/2014/02/worlds-worst-market-timer/

Question Three: How Much to Buy

Warren Buffett, Chairman's Letter to the Shareholders of Berkshire Hathaway, 1997. The "hamburger" passage and the observation that only those about to sell should welcome rising prices.
berkshirehathaway.com/letters/1997.html

AQR Capital Management, research on "buy the dip" strategies.
Comparing an investor who deploys cash immediately against one who holds cash back for declines, the dip-waiting approach produced 18.7 percent lower ending wealth. Across 196 variations of the strategy tested over approximately sixty years, average alpha was 0.5 percent per year and only 16 of the 196 showed statistically significant outperformance. AQR characterise the approach as value investing applied at a momentum horizon.

Bonini, Shohfi and Simaan, European Financial Management (2024). An independent test of buy-the-dip strategies finding no reliable outperformance over passive investing.

Estimated cost of holding cash for opportunistic purchases: approximately 0.5 to 1.0 percent per year over most historical thirty-year periods.

Question Four: When to Sell
Edwin Lefèvre, Reminiscences of a Stock Operator (New York, 1923). The epigraph is spoken by Larry Livingston, the character based on Jesse Livermore. The book is in the public domain.
Morningstar, "Mind the Gap 2025." Published 13 August 2025.

Across more than 25,000 US open-end funds and ETFs, over the decade ending 31 December 2024, the funds returned 8.2 percent per year while the average dollar invested in them earned 7.0 percent. The 1.2 percentage point annual gap is equivalent to roughly 15 percent of the funds' aggregate total return, and is consistent with the gaps measured in the studies ending in 2020, 2021, 2022 and 2023. Funds with the most volatile cash flows showed gaps of about 1.8 percentage points; sector equity funds 1.5; and all-in-one allocation funds 0.1. morningstar.com

The challenge to Morningstar. Jon A. Fulkerson, Bradford D. Jordan, Timothy B. Riley and Qing Yan, "Bad Timing Does Not Cost Investors 15% of Their Funds' Returns: An Examination of Morningstar's 'Mind the Gap' Study" (2026). Using the same sample, the authors find that poor timing specifically costs investors approximately 0.10 percent per year, and that much of the measured gap reflects the arithmetic of cash flows rather than investor error.
papers.ssrn.com/sol3/papers.cfm?abstract_id=4904652

A Note on Figures

Market data changes. Interest rates, inflation figures, fund fees and index returns cited in this book were accurate at the time of writing and will not be accurate indefinitely. Where a specific number matters to a decision you are making, look it up rather than trusting a book.

That is, in a sense, the whole argument.

FULL DISCLAIMER

General

The information provided in this book, The Gap, is for educational and informational purposes only. It is intended to give a general understanding of investment principles and strategies, and it should not be considered financial advice.

The author and publisher make no representations or warranties of any kind, express or implied, about the completeness, accuracy, reliability, suitability, or availability of the information, products, services, or related graphics contained in this book for any purpose. Any reliance you place on such information is strictly at your own risk.

No Financial Advice and No Advisory Relationship

This book does not provide financial advice. The author is not a registered financial advisor, investment advisor, portfolio manager, securities dealer, broker, financial planner, accountant, or tax professional in Canada, the United States, or any other jurisdiction, and does not hold himself out as one.

Reading this book does not create an advisory, fiduciary, client, or professional relationship of any kind between you and the author or publisher.

Nothing in this book is tailored to your circumstances. The author does not know your income, debts, obligations, time horizon, tax position, risk tolerance, dependants, or goals. Advice that ignores all of those things is not advice. Always consult a qualified professional who is aware of your individual financial situation before making any investment decision.

Not an Offer or Solicitation

Nothing in this book constitutes an offer, solicitation, or recommendation to buy or sell any security, fund, or financial instrument, nor an offer to provide investment advisory services, in any jurisdiction where such an offer or solicitation would be unlawful.

Investment Risks

Investing in financial markets involves risk, including the risk of losing some or all of the money you invest.

The value of investments can go down as well as up. Past performance is not indicative of future results. Historical returns, projections, averages, and examples used in this book are illustrative only and are not a promise or estimate of the returns you will receive.

The strategies discussed in this book may not be suitable for all investors. It is your responsibility to understand the risks associated with any investment and to determine whether it is appropriate for your circumstances.

Specific Companies, Funds, and Securities

Any reference to a specific company, stock, index, exchange-traded fund, mutual fund, or other security is for illustrative purposes only.

The mention of any specific security does not constitute a recommendation to buy, sell, or hold it. The author and publisher do not endorse or promote any company, fund, or security named in this book, and are not responsible for the performance of any of them.

The author may personally hold positions in securities of the kinds discussed in this book. Such holdings may change at any time and without notice, and no holding named or unnamed should be interpreted as a recommendation.

Accuracy and Timeliness of Information

The information in this book reflects the author's understanding of financial markets and the information available at the time of writing.

While every effort has been made to ensure accuracy, neither the author nor the publisher guarantees the accuracy, completeness, or timeliness of the contents. Financial markets, interest rates, inflation, tax rules, fee structures, product availability, and regulations change constantly, and the information in this book may become outdated. No obligation is assumed to update it.

Third-Party Data and Sources

This book refers to data, reports, and research produced by third parties. Such material is reproduced or summarised in good faith and remains the property of its respective owners.

The author and publisher do not warrant the accuracy of third-party data and are not responsible for errors, omissions, or subsequent revisions in it, or for the content of any external source, publication, or website referred to in this book.

Taxation and Jurisdiction

Tax treatment depends on your individual circumstances and on the rules of the country, province, or state in which you live, and those rules may change.

Examples in this book that refer to accounts, products, rates, or tax treatment in Canada or the United States are illustrative and may not apply to you. Nothing in this book is tax or legal advice. Consult a qualified tax professional or lawyer in your own jurisdiction.

No Assurance of Results

Neither the author nor the publisher makes any assurance, guarantee, or warranty that using the information in this book will produce profitable investments, financial security, or any particular financial outcome.

Any results described in this book, including those of the author or of people mentioned in it, are specific to those circumstances and should not be taken as typical or expected.

Limitation of Liability

To the fullest extent permitted by law, in no event will the author or publisher be liable for any loss or damage, including without limitation direct, indirect, incidental, punitive, or consequential loss or damage, or any loss of data, profits, or opportunity, arising out of or in connection with the use of this book or reliance on its contents.

Reader Responsibility

You are solely responsible for your own financial and investment decisions.

By reading this book, you acknowledge that you have read, understood, and agreed to this disclaimer, and you agree to hold the author and publisher harmless from any and all claims, losses, or damages arising from your use of the information contained in it.

Severability

If any part of this disclaimer is found to be unenforceable, the remaining provisions continue in full force and effect.

About the Author

Sriram Saravanan is a Canadian personal finance author and investor base in Toronto.

He holds an MBA from De Montfort University in the United Kingdom, and he worked across India, the United Kingdom and Canada.

He is the author of three books on personal finance: "The Game of Percentage", "The Effortless Investor", and "The Gap", which together form The Investor's Trilogy with "the Gap" being the last book he intends to write on the subject.

His work, apart from Amazon, is also stocked in more than twenty retaile across continents, including Barnes & Noble, Walmart and Kepler's Books i the United States, Indigo in Canada, Waterstones and Blackwell's in the Unite Kingdom, Feltrinelli in Italy, Bokus in Sweden, Akademika in Norway, Saxo in Denmark, Bol.com in the Netherlands and Belgium, Orell Füssli and Hugendubel in Switzerland and Germany, Eslite in Taiwan, Aladin.kr in South Korea, Jarir in Saudi Arabia, Booktopia and The Nile in New Zealand and Australia.

With travels spanning more than eighteen countries, his outlook is as global as his ambitions

Connect with him on Goodreads and LinkedIn.

www.ingramcontent.com/pod-product-compliance
Lightning Source LLC
LaVergne TN
LVHW021737071126
851857LV00040B/1473